PREEN *(pri:n)*
Vb 1. (of birds) To plume and primp, to maintain (feathers) in a healthy condition by arrangement.
2. To dress or array (oneself) carefully; Primp, to prettify.

According to Justin Thornton and Thea Bregazzi, it took them all of one evening to come up with what must surely be the perfect name for a fashion brand: Preen. After all preening is what dressing up is all about. Whether it was also designed to be a cheeky wink, a knowing nod to the fashion industry's haughty self-regard and propensity for vain posturing or not, the verb has today become a byword for one of London's most respected labels.

Revered for its deconstructed tailoring, utilitarian separates, off-kilter elegance and streamlined sophistication, Preen often resists definition. As if preferring to languish somewhere between complex yet commercial, esoteric yet accessible, alluring yet androgynous, the label has for the past decade, always marched to the beat of its own drum.

In 1996, the design duo set up shop in West London's Portobello Green. It was an unorthodox start-up plan, given that they didn't at that point have any clothes to sell. Still, it wasn't long before Justin and Thea's designs were flying off the rails. Indeed right from the start, their early, one-off creations displayed many of the themes that Preen would revisit over the next decade: Victoriana, recycling, deconstruction, utilitarian clothing.

In fact, Justin and Thea have never paid the blindest bit of notice to trends. Nor do they court celebrity or kick up their heels at fashion bashes. Instead the design duo – who are partners in real life as well as fashion – spend almost every waking hour honing their lovingly crafted creations. They're also perhaps, the only fashion designers to have come from the Isle of Man. Here they grew up at opposite ends of the island (20 miles apart), meeting first at the age of 18 on an Art Foundation course. Although they both went their separate ways – Justin studied fashion at Winchester School of Art and Thea at the University of Central Lancashire, followed by a spell as a designer for Helen Storey and as a fashion stylist respectively – they reunited on a project for Storey that made them realise what they really wanted to do was work together on their own label.

As sinuous and severe as Preen's obi-back shifts and tailored, hourglass jackets might appear, the label is, at its heart, a decidedly female-friendly one. Indeed many of the garments are designed in such a manner that they can be tied, draped, loosened, cinched or folded in a myriad of ways. It's an in-built versatility that is borne out of an understanding that their customers' needs come in all different shapes and sizes.

Enhancing the multifunctional nature of their designs, Preen's garments are also constructed as hybrids of one kind or another. Whether it's a Crombie coat with a bustle in the back; a silk camisole fused together with fluttering layers of shirt collars; or a plunge-neck swimsuit spliced together with a classic men's shirt. That such a deconstructive approach displaces many of the original garments' functional design details (transforming them into pure ornamentation), would appear to be all part of the fun.

In spite of the fact that tailored menswear has always acted as a launch pad for their women's pieces, it wasn't until S/S 2003 that the couple actually found time to design their own menswear line. The result is designs for both sexes that employ a fastidious reworking of classic menswear pieces such as a trench coat, a blazer, a crisp men's shirt. By furthermore contrasting opposites (masculine and feminine, ornamental and utilitarian), Thea and Justin seem to be exploring the nature of what makes a garment iconic. The upshot is a new dialect of clothing that is inherently modern.

That Preen's latest designs – all sculptured, draped silk dresses, pinafore-front, cubist-graphic shifts, tailored, cocoon coat dresses – are the culmination and consolidation of themes that have preoccupied Thea and Justin for the past decade, is of no doubt. However, by responding to the changing undulations in the fashion landscape, the couple have steered their label clear of its former gritty, urban deconstructionism in favour of something altogether more chic. While Thea and Justin are still doing their thing with slithers of recycled fabrics, those pieces have now evolved into fluid wrap dresses, cocktail bustiers and drapey, kimono-sleeve coats.

Perhaps this is in part due to the fact that the designers are no longer looking to historical or period references. Instead they are applying an intertextual methodology to the creative process. By deconstructing their own body of work, Preen's garments are now carefully crafted medleys of spliced together elements from previous collections.

Of course, if there were one factor that has unified Preen's collections over the past ten years, it would have to be its love affair with Victoriana. But, having explored every which way with a puffed sleeve, the two have in recent years, honed their handwriting. Increasingly, they've pared back the decoration and original ornamentation that typified their label, reducing any references to Victoriana to the mere hint of a peplum silhouette or rise of a discreet bustle. In many ways, by toning down their signature, it is now resounding more deeply than ever before.

- - - - - - - - - - - - - - - - - -

CAT CALLENDER
August 2006

This book is a personal record of our journey through the first 10 years of Preen. Compiled of images, sketchbooks, photos, personal items and moments that we have collected throughout the decade.

- -

Justin Thornton and Thea Bregazzi

FLIGHT OF FANCY

Spring Summer 1997

- - - - - - - - - - - - - - - - -

Elizabethan costume is given a rock and roll attitude in this first Preen collection.

JUMBO JET

Autumn Winter 1997/8

- - - - - - - - - - - - - - - - - -

Drain pipe trouser suits in glazed and duotone taffeta are worn over high neck herring bone bodices with delicate frilled edging and transparent cut outs. Feather encased silk chiffon shirts are worn with tight flounce hemmed mini skirts.

POST MODERN SLEAZE

Spring Summer 1998

- - - - - - - - - - - - - - - - -

East village rock and roll meets punk Victoriana. Tight bleached denims, puff sleeves and feather prints.

Preen bring you their
Autumn/Winter 98/99
dressed edwardian beauties, pulled and dragged into turn of the century
This is the uniform of
ftly flecked woollen suiting crafted to form the long lean silhouettes of the past - then pushed
shadows on soft stains of colour fall from drawstringed fine gauge knits. The cold harshness of slate

lection The Beautiful and Bedraggled
wn town New York.
own town romantic, tough and sexy, elegant and snagged, beautiful and bedraggled.
If you would like more information or to view the collection, please contact Justin on 0181 968 1542
nd tucked for the future Smart crisp cotton shirts have been split hitched and ruffled Sheer
ross fleeces are softened with gentle frills Water resistant Oxford drill give classic styles a hard edge

PIONEERS

Spring Summer 1999

- - - - - - - - - - - - - - - - -

This collection was inspired by the American pioneers and the influence of the Native American Indian costumes.

EMPIRE STATE OBSERVATORIES
1909960

"Snobbery & decay"
the concept of
tailoring
fabrics
to create

SNOBBERY AND DECAY

Autumn Winter 1999/00

- - - - - - - - - - - - - - - - - -

This was the first Preen catwalk show, held at Shoreditch town hall, and was inspired by the decline of the traditions of the aristocracy and the decay of their stately homes. Key looks were pussy bow blouses, high waisted corset belts, decaying brocade prints and the puff ball sleeve.

Satin jerseys adorned with prints of fox fur wraps
This Collection explores the decay of the aristocracy, from the glamour and decadence of the thoroughbred avant-garde, through to the sloane rangers, trustafarians and the crumbling manors of today.
Charcoal, moss and camel hunting tweeds are printed in faded brocades, combined with blush and mint. Soft fine knit lambs wool with gathered details, dropped shoulders and funnel necks. Yellow slate and steel cotton shirts are laced, puffed a
opposing fine petrol and black knit wool jersey whic
embellished with faux mink fur trim. High-tech the
are given a feminine touch with sculpted necks.
shoulders and garters. Stone, steel and olive peached
jackets are lightly quilted, skirts and trousers are p
sections of brocade. Peach, fern, camel and black sa
adorned with prints of fox fur wraps. Soft leather
bodices are edged with frills and gathers in peach, mint
Cotton shirts, laced, ruffled, puffed and gathere
Preen will be exhibiting their Autumn/Winter 1999/2000 collection at London fashion week, Tranoi Paris and holding their second catwalk show, during London fashion week.
The Preen main collection is priced from £55 to £420 and 'Preen Genes London' from £30 to £130. Available from 'Antique Boutique', New York; and 'Louis Boston', Boston; 'Rolo', San Francisco; 'Agosto shop', Tokyo; 'Michel Perry', Paris and the 'Preen shops' London and Tokyo.
Preen clientele includes Kate Moss, Honor Fraser, Tori Amos, Miranda Richardson, Liv Tyler, Janet Jackson, PJ Harvey, Sarah Cox, Natalie Imbruglia, Beth Orton, Kylie Minogue and Justine Frischman.
If you require any more information, please call Natasha on 0181 968 1542.
Preen, 5 Portobello Green, 218 Portobello Road, London, W10 5TZ
Preen, Daikanyama, Tokyo 03-3770-6175
Photography – James Muldowney 0958 752111
Make up and hair – Kim Brown 0956 27038
Model – Caitlin @ Bookings
Graphics – Nia Roberts, with thanks to Gareth
Preen Autumn/Winter 1999/2000 Collection
Snobbery & Decay
high necks.
Hunting tweeds printed with fading metallic brocades

FRAGILE FUTURE

Spring Summer 2000

- - - - - - - - - - - - - - - - -

Show venue - the old music hall on Brick lane. Edwardian time travel inspired this collection. Hand crafted leathers were moulded and sculpted to form pie crust frills. Metal chains embellish razor sharp tailoring.

TRAMP CHARINGTON

Autumn Winter 2000/1

- - - - - - - - - - - - - - - - - -

Show venue - Truman brewery on Brick lane, in a cavernous freezing warehouse. Red, pink and gold silk tulles and Scottish tweeds were combined with urban sports wear and punched leather separates, inspired by Ziggy Stardust meets Dynasty.

AW 2000/01
TRAMP CHARINGTON

PERFECTLY PERFECT

Spring Summer 2001

- - - - - - - - - - - - - - - -

Shown at Sloane terrace church hall and inspired by a Victorian haberdashery shop and the 'Virgin Suicides' film. Delicate sepia toned ruffled dresses were encrusted with an eclectic mix of diamante pearls, keys and antique trinkets. Delicate summer floral cottons were ripped and woven into tops and dresses and worn with muted leathers. There was an injection of pure rock and roll with 'spray on' pvc pants.

EXTRA ORDINARY

Autumn Winter 2001/2

The theme was Dickensian street urchins and ordinary London people. Button embellishments came from the pearly kings and queens, ragged tail coats and gathered sleeves ran throughout this collection.

SPECTACLE

Spring Summer 2002

- - - - - - - - - - - - - - - -

This show was held in the British Fashion Council tent at the Natural History Museum. Hanging above the catwalk were over 100 different birdcages. Circus performers of old inspired delicate tatters of sequin jet beading and ring master jackets.

Preen Show
'Spectacle'
17th September
6.30 pm at the
West lawn tent
en Show
pectacle'
September
at the
West lawn

Photography - Jean-Francois Carly

REFUGE

Autumn Winter 2002/3

- - - - - - - - - - - - - - - - - -

Show venue - Porchester Hall. Military inspiration transpires into suede jump suits and pocket pinafore dresses. Delicate cobweb strung pearl belts accessorise voluminous silk jersey evening dresses. There were strong recycled elements to this collection, in the form of patchwork army gillets.

bueno
preen
A/W 2002/3 show
19th february 3:45 pm
porchester hall
R.S.V.P concrete pr 0207 434 4333

FUNCTION

Spring Summer 2003

- - - - - - - - - - - - - - - - -

This show was held in New Covent Garden Market, with a 200 metre long catwalk and huge glitterballs. The inspiration was builders and ballrooms, workwear was fused with 50's inspired ballgowns. Silver lame bib and brace gave way to flowing layers of tule.

Photography - Dan Smith
Styling - Jo Adams

Photography - Tim Bret-Day
Styling - Ursula Hogh

Photography - Paul Wetherell
Styling - Jodie Barnes

PROTECTION

Autumn Winter 2003/4

- - - - - - - - - - - - - - - - - -

Show venue - The Pavilion, Shepherds Bush. Hi-tec fabrics were fashioned into futuristic capes, coats and dresses, accessorised with leather skull caps and skin tight leather leggings. A Preen urban fashion army.

'Preen has consistently
reflected the subtle pulse
of London urban cool.
Their precision draping
and cutting keeps moving
every season to new heights.'

- - - - - - - - - - - - - - -

KATE PHELAN
Fashion Director -
British Vogue

Photography - Horst Diekgerdes
Styling - Venetia Scott

'I've enjoyed watching Preen develop a more and more sophisticated point of view with their ideas about modern urban dressing - and their colour sense is brilliant'

- - - - - - - - - - - - - - - - -

SARAH MOWER
US Vogue, Style.com

Photography - Tesh
Styling - Edward Enninful

Photography - Richard Bush
Styling - Lucinda Chambers

‘I don't want to give a quote about how fabulous Preen is because I want to keep them as little known as possible so they don't up and leave London town.’

HADLEY FREEMAN

Deputy Fashion Editor - The Guardian

Photography - Joshua Jordan
Styling - Lucie McCullen

VENTURE

Spring Summer 2004

- - - - - - - - - - - - - - - -

Held in the industrial setting of the disused London Post Office HQ with a 150ft raised white rubber catwalk. Performance fabrics were mixed with silks, cottons, leathers and lurex. A glam rock super hero was the theme.

YOU ARE A
Glam Rock Superhero!
FAST – FURIOUS & FOCUSED
NO STOPPING AT END OF CATWALK –

Photography - Manuel Vason
Production - Alexander Tovey

'I am always reminded, whilst sitting in a Preen show, why I am working in fashion; always challenging, always intelligent, always thought provoking and most of all, always desirable.'

JO PHILLIPS
Co-Creative Director of Cent Magazine

SEVERINE

Autumn Winter 2004/5

On the 37th floor of one of London's tallest buildings with panoramic views and fantastic natural light, this collection had a classic 1970's French movie feel, with cashmere sweaters, trench coats and silk blouses throughout.

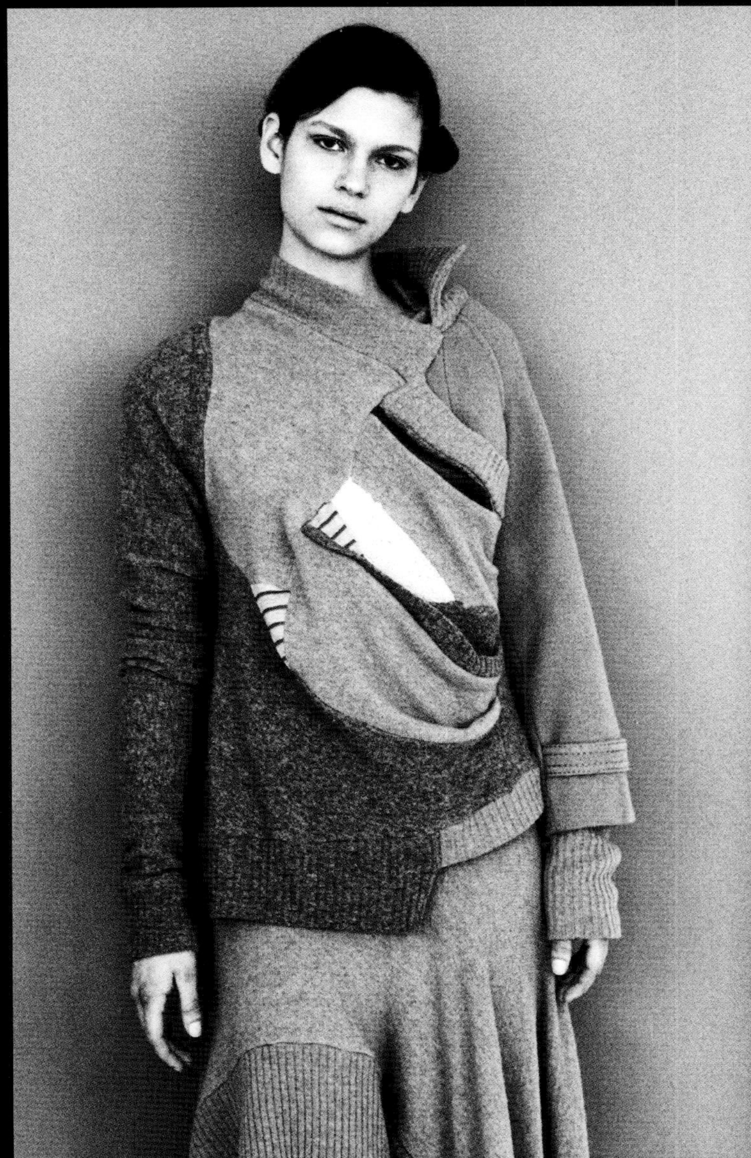

Photography - Sandra Freij
Styling - Beth Fenton

'I've had a personal affiliation with Preen for all it's years. I've watched the brand grow and funnily enough I've always wanted to wear their look. My style seems to have changed with theirs. I used to frequent their Portobello store as a young girl and wear their low waisted trousers with wing shaped pockets and velveteen backless tops to nightclubs. Now I want to be their grown up, sophisticated woman in their red cocktail dresses. I know they will continue to grow from strength to strength. I congratulate them on their tenth birthday and wish them luck for their next decade.'

- - - - - - - - - - - - -

PIPPA HOLT
Fashion Features Associate - British Vogue

AFRICAN HOBBIE

Spring Summer 2005

- - - - - - - - - - - - - - - -

Held in a vast metal floored glass office space, in the heart of the city of London, the collection took inspiration from the 1970's 'Holly Hobbie' character and African textiles, crafts and techniques.

'I love the beautiful and original way that Preen uses colour. A flush of rose here, a dusting of grey there, then suddenly a dramatic jolt of red to catch you off guard. Justin and Thea seem to know what the cool, effortlessly stylish girl really wants to wear...even before she knows herself.'

- - - - - - - - - - - - - -

KATE BLYTHE

Fashion Features Writer - Elle Magazine

Photography - Patrick Shaw
Styling - Anne-Marie Curtis

'Preen has become one of the most exciting and innovative shows in London over the past few years. I believe Justin and Thea have that unique combination that is so rare to find which is to be able to produce a visually stunning show season after season but produce clothes which women can actually wear.'

- - - - - - - - - - - - - - - - - - - -

LUCINDA CHAMBERS
Fashion Director - British Vogue

Photography - James Muldowney
Styling - Cynthia Lawrence-John

PREEN
by
thornton
bregazzi
autumn
winter
2005/6

tuesday
15th
february
3.30pm

the
great
hall

the
west
stand

stamford
bridge
football
stadium

chelsea
village

fulham
road

sw6
lhs

fulham
broadway
tube

london
fashion
week
return
bus
service
available
from
front
of
bfc
tent

name

block

row

RSVP
relativepr
@aol.com

telephone
020
7704
8866

facsimile
020
7704
8877

VACUUM

Autumn Winter 2005/6

- - - - - - - - - - - - - - - - - -

The grand hall of Chelsea football stadium was the location for this show. A massive white box was installed and harsh graphic shadows fell across the catwalk. This was a very personal collection as it was inspired by Thea and Justin's own child hood, growing up in fishing villages in the 1970's. Volume and oversized shapes were key.

AT THE END OF

FOCUSED

BE STRONG DIRECT,

R.A.P

Spring Summer 2006

- - - - - - - - - - - - - - - - -

In the Norman Foster designed London City Hall chamber with views across the Thames, a white disc of a catwalk was suspended. Light and clean, this space was the perfect setting for this collection of wrapping and twisting in washed silks, cashmere's and gabardines, with a pallet of nudes, greys and stone.

Photography - Richard Bush
Styling - Sarah Richardson

Photography - Lachlan Bailey
Styling - Charlotte Pilcher

DIMENSION

Autumn Winter 2006/7

Held in the vast modern venue 'Cardinal place' in Victoria, the models stormed down a curved white super long catwalk. This collection took inspiration from 50's couture shapes and a 1997 photograph by Mario Testino. The blonde of her hair, the red of her coat, the grey of the sky were the pallet and mood of this very modern and sexy collection.

'At last Preen is receiving the attention it deserves. Having honed their handwriting over the past decade, Justin and Thea's signature minimalist deconstruction has resulted in some of the most sophisticated, draped, wrapped dresses and precision-cut coats for A/W 06.'

CAT CALLENDER
Fashion Writer

Photography - Richard Bush
Styling - Sarah Richardson

THE SMITHS

PREEN D.I.Y.
956
RETAIN THIS CHECK
26 FEB 2005
956
PREEN
NR18

Thanks to all who have played their part in this 10 years of Preen

- - - - - - - - - - - -

Ricky & all at Agosto
Juliette Larthe
Sarah Richardson
Justine Fairgreive
Haruko Tanaka
Jasmina Sarkic
Sally Graveling
Kim Brown
Mark Thomson
Sidone Barton
Rory Wykes
Nia Roberts
Caren Westwell
James Muldowney
Dan Smith
Olivier Van De Velde
Charlotte Stockdale
Susan Bender
Richard Bush
Emma-Jane Taylor
Bianca Fincham
Philip Stevens
Alexandra Stretti
Lucy Ewing
Mark Keen
Sally Rankin
Omar
Paul Williams
Emma Plastica
Vivienne Zarvis
Hitomi Yoshii
Tomas J
Jo Simpson
Nic Jottkandt
Ingela O
Gordon King
Irena
Simon Berkavitch
Ross Sterling
Steve Savage
Mums and dads & family and friends

Credits

- - - - -

Page 3 - Photography Steve Savage
Page 4 - Ph Steve Savage,
Invite graphic design Nia Roberts
Page 5 - Ph Steve Savage,
book ph Caren Westwell
Page 6 & 7 - Graphic Design Nia Roberts,
ph Preen studio
Page 8 - Top 4 ph Steve Savage,
Bottom 3 ph James Muldowney
www.jamesmuldowney.com
Page 10 - Graphic Design Nia Roberts
Page 11 - Ph James Muldowney
Page 12 - Graphic Design Nia Roberts,
ph James Muldowney
Page 13 - Ph James Muldowney
Page 14 - Ph James Muldowney
Page 20 & 21 - Ph James Muldowney
Page 23 - Ph James Muldowney
Page 24 & 25 - Ph James Muldowney,
Catwalk ph - Ross Sterling
Page 27 - Ph Jean-Francois Carly
Page 28 & 29 - Ph James Muldowney,
ph Dan Smith, represented by
A and R Photographic
Page 30 - Colour ph James Muldowney,
B & W ph - Dan Smith
Page 31 - Ph Dan Smith, *Styling* Jo Adams
Page 33 - Ph Tim Bret-Day,
Styling Ursula Hogh
Page 34 - Ph Paul Wetherell,
Styling Jodi Barnes
Page 35 - Backstage ph James Muldowney
Page 37 - Ph Horst Diekgerdes,
Styling Venetia Scott
Page 38 - Ph Tesh, *Styling* Edward Enninful
Page 39 - Ph Richard Bush,
Styling Lucinda Chambers
Page 41 - Ph Joshua Jordan,
Styling Lucie McCullen
Page 42 & 43 - Ph Dan Smith,
Front of House ph James Muldowney
Page 44 - Ph Manual Vason,
Production Alexander Tovey
Page 46 & 47 - Ph Dan Smith
Page 48 & 49 - Ph Dan Smith,
Styling Sarah Richardson
Page 50 & 51 - Ph Sandra Freij,
Styling Beth Fenton
Page 52 & 53 - Ph Dan Smith
Page 54 & 55 - Ph Dan Smith,
Styling Sarah Richardson
Page 56 & 57 - Ph Patrick Shaw,
Stylist Anne-Marie Curtis
Page 58 - Ph James Muldowney,
Stylist Cynthia Lawrence-John
Page 60 & 61 - Ph Dan Smith
Page 62 & 63 - Ph Dan Smith
Page 64 - Ph Richard Bush,
Stylist Sarah Richardson
Page 65 - Ph Lachlan Bailey,
Stylist Charlotte Plilcher
Page 68 - Ph Dan Smith
Page 69 - Ph Richard Bush,
Stylist Sarah Richardson
Page 70 & 71 - Ph Preen Studio
& Personal
Page 2,9,15,17,19,22,26,40 -
Ph Full Stop Photography,
Tel 020 7168 0522
Page 4,6,7,8,10,12,20,25,29,
30,35,36 - Still life ph Hitomi Yoshii

- - - - - - - - - - - - - - - - - -

Limited edition of 1000 books.
Published by Preen by Thornton Bregazzi. www.preen.eu

- - - - - - - - - - - - - - - - - -

ISBN
0-9553842-0-6
978-0-9553842-0-2

- - - - - - - - - - - - - - - - - -

Graphic design by StudioThomson
Printed by Generation Press